Out of the Gilded Frame

To Frankie (as in Sinatra)
my beautifully talented friend. Thanks
for your support. Enjoy. Love,
Whezie

Louise Hinchenbach

Out of the Gilded Frame

Collected Poems

Louise Winchenbach

Acknowledgements:

Cover Art:
"Gus" © 2007 Ellen Vaughan
North Yarmouth, Maine

Library of Congress Control Number.: 2007941968

Winchenbach, Louise
Out of the Gilded Frame/Louise Windchenbach
p. 72
1. Poetry–General.
I. Title.

ISBN: 978-0-9722839-9-1

Published in the United States

𝄞𝖂𝕭
Just Write Books
Topsham, ME 04086
www.jstwrite.com • jstwrite@jstwrite.com

Contents

She Just Disappeared

Waiting at the Window

Dancing on the Snow

Dedication

This book is dedicated to
my teacher, Elizabeth Potter
for hauling me up off the floor of doubt
and being my champion.

To my classmates Burkie, Merry, Tim, Deb, and Cynthia
for everything that happened in that room upstairs.
Thanks for helping prepare these poems.

To Nancy who helped me take back my power.

To my father, Eugene, and my ex-husband, Paul. They took a
few hits in the writing of these poems, but through my
experiences with them I became a stronger woman.

My praise to God for His inspiration,
and for putting these colorful people in my path.
He teaches me to surrender each day.

Note from the Publisher

Louise came to me to put together some of her poems to give to her family and friends for Christmas. I told her that I wasn't the person nor was Just Write Books the kind of business to do that; but when I read her poems I wanted to read more. I asked her to give me all the poems that she thought should be in her book. I was expecting to find several that were not up to the standard of the few samples that were shared at our first meeting. I read each one.

I was pleasantly surprised. These poems deserve to be read widely.

Then I had to face a problem. Most poets do not create a chapbook to be published until they have had work published in journals, magazines and other publications. I even called Maine's first poet laureate, Kate Barnes, to get her opinion.

Kate has been most kind to this fledgling publisher in words and time. Kate assured me that I would make the right decision and that she would not tell me what I should do even though I had requested her advice.

Her final words were, "Nancy, you'll never get in trouble for publishing good poetry."

Taking that to heart and remembering that I never have colored within the lines or followed the dictates of the establishment in my life or work, I proudly offer this first book of poetry by Louise Winchenbach. I'm certain that you will enjoy it.

Nancy E. Randolph
Publisher, Just Write Books

She Just Disappeared

Sightings

images in grey matter trenches
march into the present
to appear on paper
deformed but brave
like tattered soldiers

each finding their place in line
standing straight and tall
they await your inspection
be kind
bayonets sheathed
guns shouldered

know me
through my battles
this is my long journey home
walk it with me
and we'll be delivered together

Quiet Places

the massive door
screeches
unoiled
against metal track
sun infiltrates
rutted, dusty floor
rectangular light stretches
toward the steel blade
resting against
split wood
it whispers to the children
behave

the winch
used to haul deer
upside down
swings in the wind
that enters with me
ancient smells
dust, kerosene, animal hides
stop me mid-step
the room is cold
I breathe out
frozen apparitions
from heated breath

one
cobwebbed window
denies
prying eyes
a view of his chamber
blocked by
half-empty paint cans
burlap bag remnants

he can do things
in these quiet places
the stillness permeates
my bones
the wind moves
through black cracks
chilling my memories

I study his instruments
vice grips
stretching wires for muskrat pelts
buck horns, thirty inches across,
eight points
pheasant feathers, wing and tail
rusty nails through plumage
leg hold traps
gonads of animals long dead
untouched ten years

Pammy

her tiny seat
was in front of mine
in first grade
Pammy had
buck teeth
with big spaces between
thick glasses that magnified her eyes
wire hair
brave on a skinny neck

dirty brown shoes
hard cracked leather
broken lace
no socks
toe-to-toe
with my shiny loafers
bright copper pennies in each slit
she wore a
pilled wool sweater
even on the warmest fall day
that smelled dusty and old

Christmas approached
Mummy knit her a periwinkle blue
headband
that tied under the chin
to cover her ears and wire hair
soft with a white angora stripe
matching mittens
like the red set
I wore with my red plaid coat
velveteen collar

I wrapped them in Santa paper
with a 5&10 cent store
green bow
I wrote
to Pammy, love Louise
in first grade scrawl

she opened the package slowly
studied
her Christmas present
through dirty glasses
she smiled so slightly
then turned back to her desk
that was good enough for me

the next day I looked for Pam
in periwinkle blue
she took off her grey wool coat
bare handed
hung it on the lowest peg
placed a crumpled paper bag
on my desk
Momma said I can't keep these

my second grade seat
was three rows from Pam
I lost track of her
sped through middle school
then high school
left behind the little girl
with thick glasses

she knew
hat or no hat
we would never be friends
she remained in the dust
like her little hard cracked shoes
with the broken lace
she just disappeared

To the Bottom of the Sea

she sits on a rickety wooden step
a chubby five year old
sticky hands clutching a cherry popsicle
that drips down
bruised, dirty legs
cherry liquid from knee
to raggedy red print shorts
hand-me-downs
too big for her small frame

oppressive heat
sweat beads
above her lip
grass-stained bare feet
tap out contentment
on cool, flat fieldstones
to the click of cicadas
summer sound

in a walkway that curves
toward the dirt drive
an old '39 Chevy rests
dull powder blue with burnt umber rust
dented round fenders
visor hood
a calico mother cat
sleeps atop the front tire

she sits before a Maine cape
that shows its age
peeling paint and lopsided buildings
a bumpy road
that *should* cause cars to slow
winds by the house
junky trucks
rattle past
everything loose and wired on
windows rolled down
elbows jutting out
trying
to find relief from the heat

her tan and white
spaniel mutt
Laddie Dog
sits by the girl's side
encircled by her arm

panting to cool his fur coat
pink tongue cushioning
hot breath
that mixes with the ninety-degree heat
awaiting his chance
to lick the sticky syrup from her skin

Mother's rock garden
her panorama
a multicolored quilt of blossoms
bees, butterflies, and hummingbirds
flit from bee balm to phlox
she watches mesmerized
contemplating a future hunt
the intended prey
snagged in a Jif jar
air holes hammered into the cover

just steps away
on the other side of the wooden screen door
Mummy is busy canning peas and beans
picked that morning
from the gardens out back
sometimes
the little girl picks buttercups
Queen Anne's Lace
and goldenrod
worries
what if she dies
leaves me behind
with him

lying side-by-side
next to the step
where she sits
her father's rubber
hip boots
smell of downriver
fish, bait and saltwater
remind her
that lobsters die in boiling pots
and crabs
pierced alive
strung in his wooden traps
sink to the bottom of the sea

Screen Door

I love the sound
of a screen door
slamming shut.
Not the aluminum
air-pressured
click kind
but the
wooden model
that rattles the front hall
and makes Mummy yell
Don't Slam That Door!

Excited kids
can't hear their own noise
on the way to
a popsicle.
Breathless,
they assault
the screen door
with sticky hands.
It whacks the side of the house
coiled metal
stretching, twanging
beyond its limit.
In slow motion the coil tightens
the door swings inward
hauled shut
wood against wood
everything snapping into place.

My cottage
has a screen door
battered wood, chipped paint
small holes in the screen
from a cat's stretch.
Charcoal grill smells drift in
laughter out.
Sometimes
I let it slam really hard
as I go in and out
six years old again

Action Figures

the child in me
believed
my father's words
obeyed his orders

he was an army man
sergeant at arms
with stripes
and a chip on his shoulder
he couldn't leave the battlefield behind
so we fought alongside

now I'm an action girl
needing a little
hand-to-hand
with G.I. Joe

I've battled and lost
over and over again
the flag I fly
is red for danger
not white for surrender

battle-weary soldier
how did I live through the war
that raged
in my home?
my marriage?
I gave away
my heart
to the first
charismatic commander
who enlisted me

Cut by Wire

we fawn over
the clay pot
examine the artist's
vibrant blues
metallic cobalt
fired at cone nine
twenty-three hundred degrees Fahrenheit
then cooled
to a glazed shine
an idol set upon
my Chinese Chippendale armoire

imagine
in Burundi Africa
holocaust refugees
gather at our coming
the cold clay pot is placed
into warm hands
brown eyes widen above a taut belly
the boy tilts the vase
peers inside
places it carefully by his father's grave

cobalt blue is lost
to the sand
that drifts across the desert
arid winds swirl
in the hollow of the vessel

Rural Processing

the child watches
the headless body
run and flop
watches the final moments
trying to stay out of his way

tough hands reach for leathery legs
plunge the body into hot water
plucking feathers
his wedding band flickers gold
as steam fogs around the man's face

he slits the lower belly
with sharpened Randall knife
removes entrails
finally severing legs and feet

puppies drowned in burlap bags
a doe swings from barn's rafter
her vacant eyes watch the child
a terrified dog held down
choked, beaten
struggling to breathe
the man raged
The child watches
backing up slowly
trying to stay out of his way

he tosses the hen
into the sink
washes the blood from his arms
the smell of Ivory and Old Spice
mix with sage and onions

Gee Gory

Normie loves to remember
his cousin
Corty Brackett

he never ever swore
he always said
Gee Gory

When we was tied up in Gloucester
sometimes he'd make two trips
to The Old Howard in Boston
I furrowed my brows
perplexed

Normie and Pudge
recalled their days of burlesque
with a smile
Pudge winked
Not that I ever saw it myself
My older brother told me

Corty
would grab a couple of cigars
hop a train to Boston
hang out at
The Old Howard
three doors down from
Casino Burlesque
across from The Cave
in the combat zone

tassels and thongs
loud saxophones
Fleischmann's whisky
some dollar bills
to hand out
he'd wind his way back
to the train
through clusters of hookers
who wanted to know Corty
a little better

He'd come back
aboard the boat
and say
Gee Gory!
What a show
What a show

then he'd jump right on the train
go right back
and see it again

Button Fish

Normie, old now
holds the toy boat
cut from oak block
ax-hewn and whittled
by an *Ole fisherman 'thuther side of the harbor*
painted flat white
gaff-rigged
jigger sail
Ta hold 'er into the wind
for daydream fishin'

as a boy
he'd push the ship through
a sea of braided rug
circle the coffee table
settin' his nets
swing the boom's tiny woven basket
out over woolen waves
to scoop up his fish

My mothe'd cut buttons off everything
shirts, dresses, coats
She never threw nothin' away
She had a Velvet Tobacco can full of 'em
small white buttons
leather, bone, rhinestone
Navy pea coat buttons

They was my fish

Scattered

In the wake
of my father's wrath
my mother
sister
and I
left scattered
over the floor
wooden toy soldiers
eyes open
long after
he'd left the room

Berry Pickers

Sun warms our backs
my sister and I concentrate
filling our buckets
with September blackberries
seedy sweet
off the bush

thorns grab my pants
tug at my sleeve
objecting to
my thievery
I reach under
clustered green leaves
turning red in the fall wind

a fat berry drops
into the tangled growth
beneath my feet
heavy boots
snap thicket branches
as I push deeper into
the briars
forgetting my eventual
retreat

artists return from the cliffs
stop along the rocky path
drop their easels
next to blackberry patch
frame us in fingered boxes
envisioning
a Homer painting
rose madder
thalo blue shirts

oils forgotten on the path
one artist asks
Which berries do I pick?
Are the red ones o.k.?
my sister
scoops some
from her bounty
fills his hand
we watch him
feel the berry
taste the black sugar

we linger
reluctant to leave
spot a new patch
plow deeper into the nettles
and clustered berries
communicants
among plucky bushes

forty years gone
my sister and I
remember
childhood
berry pickers
back to school
yellow buses
stained fingers and faces
Mummy close by
preparing the jam
we'll spread
on our winter toast

Pebble Beach Rocks or When is Enough, Enough?

my pockets sag from the pull of pink quartzite
black, grey, gilded mica stones, salt and pepper granite
with deep striations
tumbled smooth by the sea
I dip them in tide pools to test their values
they clack together
as I move from the water's edge
to my sorting place above Pebble Beach

years before
barefoot and sixteen
I wandered over these same stones
dreaming of Island boys
whose kiss I would enjoy later that night
I spread my hands over texture
closed my eyes
a man could not feel better
could not be this strong
or smooth or hot

I want to take them home
Quartzite, Feldspar, Basalt, Roxbury Pudding Stone
load them with a backhoe that beeps when it backs up
onto a wagon pulled by a team of Clydesdales
shaggy fur over giant hooves thudding over the dirt path
over roots and ruts
they'd haul that wagon down to the dock
massive weight controlled
with a tug of leather through my fingers

I could bring a barge from Boothbay
ten miles over rolling waves
to scoop my stones into the jaws of the crane
onto the floating scow that settles deeper
as I find the tonnage
that feels like enough

but then...
the sea reminds me
see the vastness before you?
it cannot be held or captured

I gather a few of my favorite stones into plum fleece
head back up trail number one
to my cottage
with yellow crescent moon shutters

Waiting at the Window

The Sentinel

my sneakers
slowed on black tar
seconds passed
I tried to focus
on the empty space
where the elm once stood

the four-foot stump remained
pitiful at my feet
limbs
scattered about
woodchips
littered the mossy ground
sawdust
in muddy tire tracks
told the story

the sentinel
had shaded mourners
in the tree-lined cemetery
protected delicate moss and German ivy
that wove through headstones
granite posts leaned left and right
marking the entrance
where Anna May Simmons
had waited
since 1824
blanketed in pink phlox

halted by a chainsaw's bite
the elm
was brought down
by a man
who would move away
months later
with pocket money
for Budweiser and Winstons

Clay Tigers

boys are clay tigers
twisting in my palm
grey and hard and pliable
flatten them
form them again
into lions
or wolves
pinch their mane into being
they roar, heads thrown back
wolf eyes wink at me
gnashing teeth saber over soft lips
and then devour
all that I am

Waiting at the Window

darkness
on wet streets
yellow beams
reflecting rivers

counting cars
counting seconds
between street lamps
they pass

the pendulum swings
in slow rhythm
where is he?
where is he?
where is he?

I take attendance
at my window
every driveway has a car
every house has a husband
except mine

waiting at the window
fifteen years
twenty years
three o'clock
four o'clock
tick-tock
tick-tock

I pace
window-to-window
check my babies
my thoughts run away from me
flickering then pushed deep
like a salmon on the line
fighting under the surface

morning
cars drive down
the tree-lined street
I can see their colors now
lemon yellow
slick red
as the sun settles upon their rooftops

Wolf Spirit

medicine man
at my kitchen table
Kelloggs in blue willow
held by ancient hands
tobacco stained
hardened
spotted brown

I circled the table
never moving my eyes from him
beaded headdress
eagle feathers
fell across
a face centuries wrinkled
two deep scars maimed
his eyebrow, cheekbone
crossed a useless opaque eye

he did not speak
but rose motioning
for me to follow
moccasins on linoleum
out my back door
we walked to the lake
sun reflecting on Squam waters
alternating breaths

Chief Bravewolf finally spoke
the wolf walks by your side
she is always there
she is your sister
sit quietly, woman
listen to your spirit

he turned
walked back toward the camp
moccasins on damp moss
dissipating
all that remained
were spongy footprints
and a spirit I had not known

Small Town Bugs

the bugs
are out tonight
flying
up through my high beams
moths
the size of apples
pop like acorns
against my windshield
kamikaze warriors
determined
to end it all
in the village of Hancock

Father's Day

your first born
blue hot light
nebula forming
within your black space
a new energy
distant, fierce

asleep in the sun by the sea
baby across your chest
matching breaths
unfolding you
from the tight box
you'd become

you must have wanted
to slip behind the wheel
of your MG
head South or West
anywhere
you could live like a king
alone

I never asked
what price you paid
our hands always out
like unfeathered birds
hungering

Bartering

the gull stands on granite ledge
above me
Share that Cheeto
with me
I'll tell you a secret

orange fingertips
hold the Cheeto
stretch toward him
he says
This requires trust
I say
So does keeping a secret

he sidles down the ledge
clumsy on the ground
beady eye upon me
steals it
from my fingers
like a thief
swallows it whole
then laughs
beak to the sky
You can't control anything...
freedom is in the letting go

I'm disappointed
That's not much of a secret
he says
Maybe not
but it's a lesson you need to learn

he expects more Cheetos
promises more secrets
I lick my fingers clean
crumple the bag
shove it into my backpack

rising like a helicopter
he hovers off the cliff
a slight dip of his left wing
drives him to the surf below

A Poplar Notion

sixty feet above me
poplar leaves
rustle
mingling
waiting for the wind

they chatter about
sunshine
birds and blight
the wind picks up
they start to cheer
excited
waving
turning light-to-dark
as they flip
on their stemmed feet
front-to-back

my daughter joins me
side-by-side
we stretch
in lime green
South Beach chairs
I point out the leaves
she says
I feel a poem coming on
I smile
Nobody wants to hear
about milling poplars
nobody wants to hear
about trees
or the quiet work they do

her words carry
on the wind
above us
through branches
and sprightly leaves
I want to hear about it

From Here to Paris

I sit on the edge
of a granite jetty
two hundred feet
above a jeweled sea
sun face on
wind brushing hair
into my eyes
I work the pieces back in place

How can this be such a beautiful day?
my mother will soon be gone
there's nothing I can do
there's nothing between me and Paris
except the ocean and

eiders
floating on patterned spume
awaiting migration
limboed
on pale green swells
that spread over grey rocks

preening
soft feathers of grey
hair
that fall
across pink cables
my mother bides her time
riding
on waves
of opiate sleep
I study her exhaustion

soon she will return
to Paris
or
to the cliffs where I wait
to embark upon a new journey
her soul will
choose
another life, another path
repeating the pattern
eternally

Old Blue Eyes

I drew my scarf tighter
trying to become more compact
adjusted clothing
to cocoon myself against the cold

surprised by a young man
sitting on the sidewalk
unshaven
apathetic
backed against concrete and steel
gloveless hands held out
a Starbucks coffee cup
asking for whatever I could spare

how could I avoid this?
uncomfortable with his youth
his plight
I searched my left coat pocket
my right hand struggled with shopping bags
Christmas prosperity
in neat packages

a dime and two pennies
the sum of my pockets
he teased, *Pennies gratefully accepted*
I tossed in my coins
avoiding his eyes
quickened my step

my destination
was warm and inviting
a church filled with people
warm in their furs
comfortable in their situations
soon
I'd be among the congregation
complacent in my pew

he should have been a memory
but a block from the church
I shuffled the packages
and surveyed the contents

of my other pocket
a surprised hand retrieved
two crumpled dollar bills
my pace slowed
without permission
my feet stopped
turned
took me back
toward the young man

his familiar lament
Whatever you can spare
was light in the cold night air
people passed
gaze averted
toward the street
replaying my behavior

lifting the cup in my direction
his peacock blue eyes
locked onto mine
I studied the face
I had avoided
on the first pass
his smile widened

I wished him a
Merry Christmas
made my deposit
his eyebrows lifted
And a very Merry Christmas to you, too

Where the Pavement Ends

We hit the dirt
gravel snapping
metal undercarriage
Oh Shit!
braking
swerving
out of control

angry people honk
yelling
She needs narcotics
She's not eating
Two more nodules in the lung
God
What are they saying?
What the hell happened to the road?
the pavement just ended
without any warning

out of the car
I walk back
to look for the signs
Christ
they're fluorescent orange
five feet by five feet
PAVEMENT ENDS
CANCER
STOP

Permission to Come Aboard

the Candy B II
chugged through the harbor
forty-six feet of grey and white grace
hot pink bumpers lined her side
the setting sun sparkled her wake

Captain Normie Brackett
nudged Candy past moorings
as the crew scurried around the deck
carrying thick ropes
to tie up to the dock
adjusting bumper ties

we grabbed our guitars
Boone's Farm apple wine
ran the dirt road to the wharf
out of breath we scanned
the pilot house for Normie

boys in yellow oilskins
with sideburns
and thick weathered hair
clomped the deck in
black hip boots
smiled up at us
the crow's nest rocked
away from the dock
and in again

half way down the ladder
I heard his laugh behind me
a space between front teeth
marked his smile
a Camel cigarette pinched
between index finger and thumb
don't you know you're supposed to ask permission
to board a boat?

I squinted
studying his face
he looked playful
Permission to come aboard Captain?
He took a long drag of the camel
chuckled as he nodded
Christ, yes, Come aboard and have a hake!

Hardened Heart

my father tossed boulders
through open wounds
into my small chest
horse's ass
Goddamned dumb head
cemented hard

the words kept pinging
around my head
at the dinner table
I swallowed hard
to force them
down my dry throat
they took a hideous turn
to my heart instead
and hardened there

broken people
casually
tossed in pebbles
like pennies into a wishing well
their bitters became
my mountain

the child inside me
took an ax
began to break apart
the cement block

chunks
fell away
with each blow
the conglomerate
fifty years
heavy in my chest
gave way
to rock and gravel and dust

Angel connected me
to a Father
who churned
debris to a honey thick flow
softening my heart until
it started to beat

liquid love
pulsed onto journal pages
line by line
across pure white paper
to safely harden into words

lighter and lighter
my breathing eased
a Spirit
Holy and strong took its place
peace settled
where mortar had been

one father broke me
like a colt with a harness and bit
one Father touched my heart
and set me free

Don't I Dread It

we gather
below deck
around the fold-up table
in the galley
sisters singing
folk songs
men telling sea stories
sweet harmony
to the roll of a vessel

the fishermen listen
Francis from *The Crow*
Clyde from *The Lou Ann*
sit cockeyed
boat shoes tapping
boys curl in the berths
smoking
ice cubes
clinking between songs

the boats
rafted three abreast
from the dock
bump together
making us all sway
from swells and whisky

after a few songs
Francis pours three fingers
of Jim Beam
for the third time
humming to the music

Normie lights up
studies his crew
shakes his head slowly
Ain't this a sight?
he knows his men won't fish
tonight
maybe not tomorrow either
he pours another Fleischmann's
chuckles as he rests his arm
across his belly
I gutta get drunk tonight
and don't I dread it

Icky

wretched cat
loping from the back
of the general store
dispirited eyes, dimmed over years
downcast on wooden floor

unlicked
dull black fur
clumped from boney sides
shocked in all directions
an escapee from
clothes dryer hell
Stephen King's
cat
willed back from the grave
had nothing on Icky

my daughter and I
part
to make way
for the cranky cat
who
does not stop for a pat
does not rub against our legs
does not purr

he ambles
around the canned peas
heading for the front door
I turn to the cashier
Katie, whose cat is that?

asked this before
she tersely acknowledges
He's my cat
He's old and he's Icky
and that's no reason to kill him

I can't help thinking
maybe
Icky wants this over with

he continues his journey
out the front door
up the path
to his house
never
looking
back

Buzzy

Leroy grabbed the .45
as I ate my Cheerios
shot sister Connie
then brother Buzzy
as my mother tucked peanut butter and a banana
into my Roy Rogers lunchbox

Buzzy crawled through remote backwoods snow
red upon white pooled where he died
as I waited for my bus
cradled by a neighbor he begged, *"Please don't let me die"*
as I sat in the seat next to my best friend Rita
huddled in boyfriend whispers

Connie was loaded into the ambulance
by two attendants who worked on her heart and bullet holes
blue flashing lights pulled away from the crime scene
as I hung up my winter coat

the coroner approached the tarp
pulled it back
the boy's elfish, heart shaped face
stared up at him through inert eyes
as I took my spelling test
distracted by the empty desk next to mine

the hearse pulled into Waltz's Funeral Home
men stood solemn, hands folded
as Mrs. Hallowell prayed in front of her fourth grade class

I stared out the school bus window
watching the fields, rundown buildings, and junk cars pass
remembered
a book thrown in anger
that left a small scar above my mother's right eye
dinner dishes swept onto linoleum squares
as he screamed "Bitch" in her face

Leroy shot his family
I never found out why
my father's anger flooded through me
as I realized
he would kill my mother
eventually

Dancing on the Snow

Choreographed by God

a canoe slips through Squam waters
the women stop paddling
they spot him in spindly brush
grey outline on granite perch

he knows they are watching

instantly airborne
the great blue wingspan
draws him within yards
of outstretched hands
pencil legs tuck back
to form a straight line with the heron's body

he puts on a show
gliding two feet above the surface
the women squeal their delight
turbulent commotion rocks the canoe
laughter races ahead of the heron's flight

God watches
He chuckles
I dare not display my nesting loons
or they'll end up in the lake.

Aftermath

the generator
grumbles to life
thick green hose
snaking down to my cellar
sucks gallons per minute
toward metal trap
through the belly of the snake
onto the street above

sitting on warped step
I study my
flannel pj's
black and white penguins
that smile at me
from their apple-green background
my bright yellow rubber boots
pin the nozzle
to cement floor
as it tries to lift its head
toward the surface

my life
drifts in the current
shredded Christmas tree paper
a single Birkenstock
plastic party forks and spoons
athletic sock

I grab and toss
from cold clear water
swirling at the snake's mouth
grab and toss
before they're swallowed

wading to my knees
my flashlight beam
scans
submerged
furnace
suitcases
Benjamin Moore paint cans
storage bin tipped sideways
a pink turtleneck waves
its distress
then
through the beam
a sublime red orb
silver top and hook
bobs past me
resplendent
halo of light
that kindles a memory

trimming the tree
with my daughters
by the warmth of the fire

Winter Solstice

the plow
pushes up the hill
grumbling
at the early morning chore
tonnage scraping pavement
muffled chains clank
around ribbed Firestones
snow whispers to the ground
outside her window
angels are patient

her breathing stops
I hold my own
watching, listening
my fingertips find a pulse
messages to the heart
still undelivered
fade
then disappear
stillness settles
I speak my love softly
she lifts free

the following day
I run to forget
the river to the east
lifts the morning sun
I have to squint
shade my eyes in the glare
she's there
dancing on the snow
diamonds move about her feet
my running slows as I take her in
the sky is alive with the message
I breathe out *Mummy*

passing cars must wonder
at my smile
and colloquy
with the swirling snow glitter
that follows me down the road
effortlessly
to the piccolo and harp
coming from my headset
we travel side-by-side
peaceful companions
disappearing in the sun's glow

Scud Running

Clear prop
seven cylinders
fire in order
piston-to-piston
guttural engine groaning
the wind whispers
through crossed wires
let's go
he throttles forward
leaves behind
children, wife, business
finds God
scud running beneath the clouds

he swoops down upon us
mountain climbers
resting on the summit
the bi-plane's silver wings
dip toward the peak
he pedals the rudder left
banks in a wide arc
circling his silent audience
flying square
left aileron, left stick
just below cumulus ceiling
just above our heads

we turn in place
following the Waco's flight
waving both arms
unaware of our joy
we are all up there with him
flying front seat

he claims his heaven
two passes
three
twisting closer
with each maneuver
steel legs, thick rubber tires
swing out like a carnival ride

I could watch forever
but he tires
as G-force tunnel vision
closes in around him
pulling back hard on the stick
he climbs steeply
levels his flight
steers toward home

my heart aches
for the perfection
of the man
who storms without a barn
I watch him
out of sight
he becomes an eagle
hummingbird
dot

wheels squeak
rubber on pavement
the tail wheel drops gently
he steers blindly
left rudder, right rudder
back to the hangar
abandoned
on cockpit seat
leather helmet, goggles
surrendering
a spirit
he won't find again
until he throttles forward
and lifts
once more
toward the mountain ridge

Resurrection

upon his death
my father's soul
transforms
in black-rooted soil
wicking upward
through forested host
phloem and xylem layers
surrounding dead heartwood
interfuse the apparition
cell-to-cell
up the massive trunk
to its lofty crown

above the timberline
a vista
spreads before him
violet mountains
mica granite ledges glint
above switchback river
he shares his space with
a bald eagle
whose talons grip
interwoven branches
as he lands
searching for balance

my father is
at peace
no longer compelled
to level his rifle
at a doe's heart
he shelters her now
dropping leaves
for her fall bed

challenged only by the wind
he flourishes
free from judgment
and a mother
who snapped the rod
across the palm
of her cruel hand

I press my face against
patterned bark
lift my eyes to
spinning kaleidoscope
variegated canopy
of blues and greens

his arboreal spirit
sends leaves
higher and higher
into the sky

God Damn Potatoes

cocktail hour
at the fish house
end of the season
remnant tourists buy up the last
hard-shell lobsters
from Shermie's first set
a week before

tomorrow the market will close
tonight in the back room
we warm in a pinot noir
vodka martini glow
a box of Triscuits
some pickled herring
spread on a workbench

old Sherm comes through the side door
I come to get some a them mackerel
for my suppa
he bends over the tall white bucket
filled with cold sea water
fillets shimmer silver and black
as he plunges his hand
into the bucket
five or six times

Sherm is tall and thin
still handsome for his 80s
a highliner in his day
setting and hauling more traps
than anyone on the Island
a fisherman of renown
the kind of captain who
makes you feel safe
even in a storm at sea

I'm gonna boil these up
with lotsa patatas
he passes on the drink
and heads up the hill
to Barbara and the boiling kettle

he's back in ten minutes
looks at his son and says
Shermie, gimme some a them god damn patatas, will ya?
father and son
dig in the bin
bag just the right russets
then Sherm tosses them on the counter
and settles into the plastic chair
next to me
Shermie hands him
gin on the rocks
in a Flintstone's jelly glass

we listen
to sea stories
about the early Island days
how he caught a 250-pound halibut
on a fifty-pound test line
when a Boy Scout
hooked it
on a fishing trip
aboard *The Phalarope*
Ya got somethin' big on that line, son
betta let me take it
time slips by
no one leaves their chairs
no one else speaks

he jumps up
looks left then right
where'd I put them damn patatas?

he grins
the creases at the corners of his eyes deepen
with a vigorous step
he grabs the potatoes
saunters out the fish house door again
makes for the hill and Barbara

Boobs

bon bons
blockade bellies
beneath the blouse
beyond second base
bondage booty bridled
buttressed with brassiere
Beelzebub's bare bounty
blasphemous balance of power
beckon boys to bay at the moons
b-cup a-cup c-cup d-cup buttercup
bottle-blond babes bounce to the beat
befuddled boarding school boys babble
bestsellers that betray blase' bibliophiles
bourgeois buccaneers bursting over corset
bathrobes burst cleaving a bad bodacious set
baroque baseballs, basketballs baptized by beards nip
boisterous battle cry bombardiers on the battlefield ple
bewitched, beguiled and then the witch begets
brazen bovine bosoms brawl in the brothel
bachelors bedded with backstreet bribes
below the belt swing low sweet chariots
boyfriends beg to do bona fide business
below balconies banister Romeo barks
buff and brown and black bombshells
burlesque balloons tasseled and taut
baa baa black sheep two bags full
bombastic buoyant bureaucrats
Bronco Billy's bucking dyad
boulders pull on shoulders
bonneted button caps
blamed for betrayals
bikinis embrace
brass knockers
the badlands
blackmail
boy bait
behold
boobs

Monhegan Is My Purple

red rock blue sky mix
fun and eccentric
in lavender sunset
slipping over the edge of
Manana
Casket Rock

I glide back and forth
slouching deep
into the porch swing
rocking
in dahlia purple pants
plum polish encircling
crystal stem

purple-streaked hair
on the truck driver
who plays with her lip ring
puce print socks
cross at her ankles
as she stretches
on the truck's bed
waiting for the summer people
to haul their
eggplant-colored suitcases
beneath the tailgate

pomegranate sea
illuminates magenta spruce
fall ragweed waves
in violet winds
burnt umber beneath yellow

Pinot Noir
slides down easily
I warm to humanity
in their grape skins
shriveled in the sun
mauve seaweed slides
over lilac kelp
as I sip my way deeper into
the color purple

Have a Heart, Lisa

still in her street clothes
she opens one eye
scans the sunlit room
half empty vodka martini
on bedside table

Lisa'd had a good night
smooth liquor bath
mackerel fry
baiting Havahart traps
with a bottle of Cuervo Gold
a thong
and a lacey push-up bra
on the *blow-up Betty* doll

it was time
to make her famous donuts
feed the cats
check her traps

stepping out onto the porch
overlooking Fish Beach
she smiled
hands on hips
surveying
all four traps
sprung
sometime during the night

trapped
foolish boys
a blonde, two browns and a red
she'd caught
a bushy-tailed bastard
a red-headed liar
and two ring-tailed rats

rectangular men
stuffed into Havaharts
on top of deflated *Bettys*
heads twisted sideways
faces smashed against wire mesh
noses poking through
beards wisping around

the metal weave
eyes shifting side-to-side
as fingers try to reach the
release latch

blocks of boys
with fire in their eyes
what to do...
what to do...
give them to the cat to play with?
here kitty, kitty, kitty...
so many uses
a tasty soup?
a warm fur coat?
eunuchs to serve her?

she smiled
remembering a week ago, Tuesday
she and her buddy
set nets
in the harbor current
hauled in
a silver-backed cheater
a big-balled codger
a lying crappy fish
and a wide-mouthed carp
his silver tongue
pleading for release

the beach had been alive with movement
men flopping
flipping
on the sand
arms locked at their sides
mouths heaving open and closed
to catch the sea air
eyes wide in terror
or glazed quiet as they died

today was another day
she grabbed her skiff
pushed off the beach

she needed to check her nets

Lost and Found

i found it
under someone else's needs
other people's dreams
i thought someone had taken it
but i was careless
and lost it years ago

it disappeared in childhood
tucked away
with the ridicule and threats
Sit down and shut up
I'll give you something to cry about
You're a horse's ass
and shame
when i wet the bed
taunting
Piss-a- baby...piss-a- bed

it was under
heaps of affairs
dalliances
uncherished Valentines days
next to
the blame
It's your fault I acted badly
You're a cold woman

i found it
on top of the
hand-maiden gloves
Cinderella slippers
mixed in with the guilt
When a man's not happy at home...

ribbons of
you'll mess it up
let me make the decisions
wove through the mess
that would take
years to untangle

gone
all these years
found
as i removed
each layer
self- esteem
emitting
tangerine light
vibrating
like the bass of a cello
growing
louder
stronger
with each layer

I danced
when I found it
held it close
embracing
Me

The Avenger

skipping along forest path
she approaches the cottage
warm smells, homemade cookies
await her
eager to please
she lifts the latch
adjusts her basket
singsongs, *Grammy, Baby Red is here!*

the goodness of grandma swims in his belly
the little girl stands before him
he draws her in
the better to see you with…taste you with
the menacing smile widens
a basket of goodies
won't satisfy his hunger
it's her flesh
and bones
and heart he craves

turning to face the wolf
she lowers her head
bright eyes lock onto predatory ones
turn steely
Not this time, she whispers
smiling
her small hand encircles cold steel
index finger curling around
the Smith and Wesson's
familiar trigger
used earlier on the witch
at the candy-caned cottage
on the other side of the forest

all the bad ones soon shall fall
Baby Red will kill them all
tossing her weapon into the basket
she calculates
the fastest way to the Beanstalk

Chasin' Cars

Normie leaned forward
elbows on knees
hands clasped in front of him
full belly straining
against blue plaid

I studied his paratrooper tattoo
from the Korean War
on his right forearm
suddenly he chuckled
I fooled around quite a bit
when I was younger
his fourth wife
worked quietly at her computer
she smiled
seemed to know what was coming

I teased
you behavin' yourself these days?

Normie sat straight
threw his head back and laughed
as he considered his answer
Christ, yes
I'm too old now
I'm like a dog chasin' a car
wouldn't know what to do with it once I caught it

I threw back my head and cackled
his wife just shook her head

Freedom

yellow ochre eyes
scan the gallery
he smells of turpentine
titanium white plumage
wet and oily
elongate, soften to feathered wings
he lifts from the canvas
out of the gilded frame
at midnight

the studio cats
Moonie and Star
sit side-by-side
rose madder, thalo blue
smudged in calico fur
whiskers twitch
multicolored heads
move in circles
tracing the bird's pattern
they crouch with each low pass

Moonie turns back to the painting
as the female tries to follow
hopping off granite rock
squishing flecked grey paint
onto the table top
linseed oil and burnt sienna web prints
sign the visitor guest book
but the artist's shortened brush stroke
has rendered her incapable of flight

the male black back gull
careens down hallways
scanning left then right
for an escape
his instinct scolds
garbage fish bones sea urchins night air
freedom
now

pulling up toward the full moon
he slams into the Plexiglas skylight
his guttural cry pierces the stillness
stunned
he glides down to join the female
alone in the moonlit streak
on hardwood floor

touching her beak with his
they stand before the huge oil
sixty inches by fifty inches
on the floor in front of them
a bonfire scene on fish beach
tended by three Islanders
orange faces glow
sparks and stars
mix in the black sky
they can feel the heat
their feathers ruffle slightly in the breeze

he pushes off
circling in a wide arc
around the gallery's ceiling fan
then dives toward the painting
swooping into the night
clearing the fire by several inches

she waddles quietly onto the sandy beach
webbed feet on shell shards and beach glass
out to the cool ocean air
as he lifts
toward Manana
squawking
free free free

Printed in the United States
200610BV00003B/391-597/A